Stingers

Written by Jo Windsor

This bee can sting.

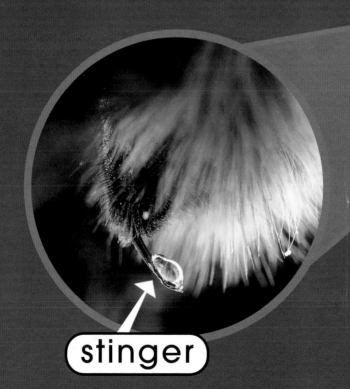

stinger

This scorpion can sting.

stinger

This wasp can sting.

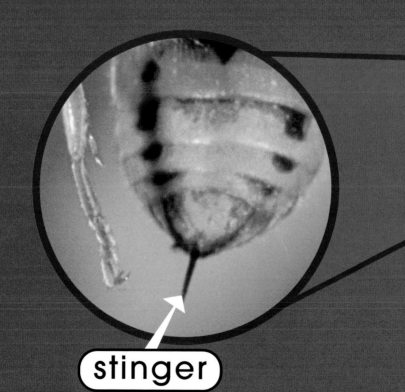

stinger

This fish can sting.

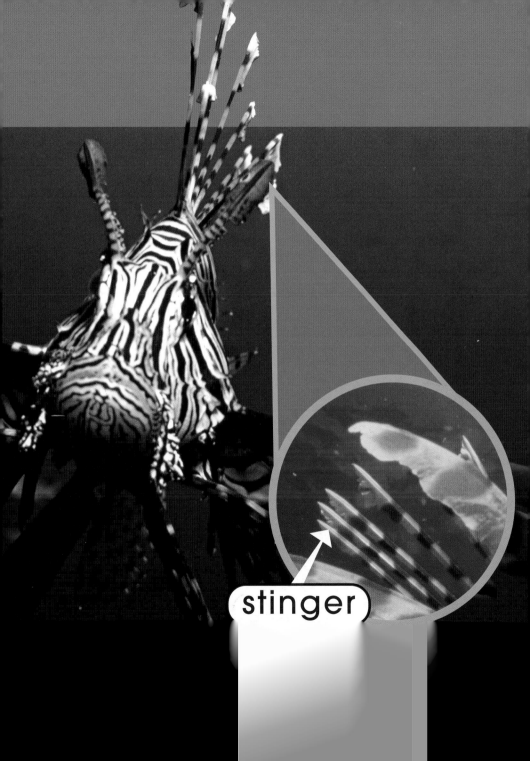

stinger

This plant can sting.

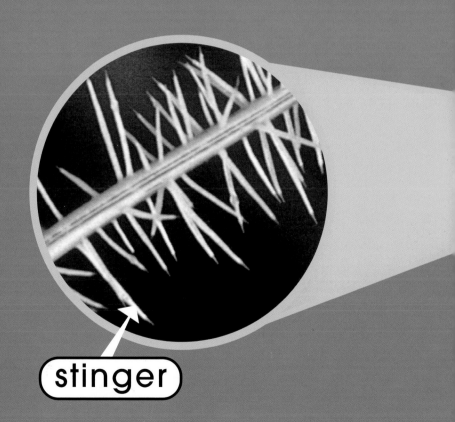

stinger

This jellyfish can sting.

stinger

Index

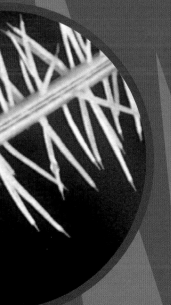

Guide Notes

> **Title: Stingers**
>
> **Stage:** Emergent – Magenta
>
> **Genre:** Nonfiction (Expository)
> **Approach:** Guided Reading
> **Processes:** Thinking Critically, Exploring Language, Processing Information
> **Written and Visual Focus:** Photographs (static images), Index, Labels
> **Word Count:** 24

FORMING THE FOUNDATION

Tell the children that this book is about animals and plants that have stingers.
Talk to them about what is on the front cover. Read the title and the author.
Focus the children's attention on the index and talk about the animals and the plant that are in this book.
"Walk" through the book, focusing on the photographs and talk about the different animals (and plant) and their stingers.

Read the text together.

THINKING CRITICALLY

(sample questions)

After the reading
- Why do you think these animals have stingers?
- What do you think would make an animal use its stinger?

EXPLORING LANGUAGE

(ideas for selection)

Terminology
Title, cover, author, photographs

Vocabulary
Interest words: sting, scorpion, wasp
High-frequency words: can, this